Duck Hunting Lake Erie
1945-1954

Bruce Barber

Published by BBarber Publishing
1727 North Wilson Ave Suite # 505
Loveland Colorado 80538
BBarberBooks@yahoo.com

Website:
www.BruceBarberBookslulu.com

ISBN 978-1-329-14205-3

In loving memory of my parents
Bea & Jack Barber,
for making my hunting years most memorable

Preface

Speaking for self and my brother John Barber,we were blessed to have a Dad who gave of himself, his time and a world of duck hunting experience that allowed us to completely enjoy every moment duck hunting together for several years. Our memory banks are filled with memories that we will forever owe to ourMom and Dad.

Mom was the greatest for tolerating the mess we brought home after each hunt, wet clothes, boots, guns and normally a few ducks which she not only helped clean but knew how to prepare wild game dinners fit for a King.

Dad set the decoys and Mom set the table and both performed their jobs very well.

May God rest their Souls

Table of Contents

Preface

Reflecting back the best years for a young boy to grow up I am ever so thankful. The post World War Two era was a time to remember,life was simple and patriotism was heavy in the air. My Dad, Jack Barber, was an avid sportsman involved in sporting organizations that were to become the foundation for sport hunting and conservation as we know it today.

Born in 1935 and a youngster during World War Two, a time when almost everybody I knew was in uniform or working in the defense industry. At the ages of seven and nine Dad would load us up and take us to the Erie County field days where we would spend the day observing skeet shooting, crow calling competition and wander around all of the neat exhibits.

We were introduced to the outdoors at very young ages and feel blessed to this day for being exposed to the good old days. Grand parents and uncles owned large farms that allowed us to fire guns and carry our BB guns into the woods on big game hunts which we normally ended up our with bagging several stumps and a few cattails.

Uncles and cousins enjoyed all aspects of the outdoors whether it was working on wildlife habitat or practicing our marksmanship skills we enjoyed a common thread for years growing up.I opted to write this book for those that missed the glory years of Duck Hunting on Lake Erie primarily on Presque Isle Bay.

I am amazed at how the sport changed so drastically in a ten year period extending from 1945 to 1955. Duck hunting remains a very popular sport and without Ducks Unlimited, NW Duck Hunters Association. and the thousands of dedicated volunteers involved in the sport there would be little to write about today. To past, present and future waterfowl hunters I salute you for your contributions to the preservation of waterfowl and the many non hunted species that benefit from hunting license sales and hands on volunteer efforts by so many.

Although Colorado pales in comparison to Lake Erie I enjoy observing and photographing ducks passing through Northern Colorado every spring and fall. Canada geese are in abundance and at the goose hunting is fantastic for those that enjoy field hunting.

I still get a rush when I see large flocks of ducks circling our many reservoirs. I have hung up my guns in favor of the camera's and feel it is a nice exchange after years of gun hunting. The only thing different is the shutter does not make as much noise as the shotguns. We have excellent snow goose hunting in the southeastern corner of the state with unlimited bag limits offering hunters a good day afield.

Bruce Barber

Chapter 1

Learning the Ropes

I enjoyed being out in the field and woods in the fall when the colors and smells were magical to me. Dad would stop and sit on a stump and break out our lunch, of which the dogs normally ended up with most of mine as I pet them and picked burrs out of their coats.

We would return home with Dad's game bag full, and that is when I was introduced to the rest of the story, cleaning game and guns. I well remember plucking feathers and blowing them out of my nose, the down was attracted to my nose which was just at table level. Mom was a real trooper, being raised in the country she learned to clean birds at a young age. It became a family affair as John joined in, at which time Dad ghosted leaving the three musketeers to pluck feathers and draw innards. John and I became avid game dressers as we anxiously awaited for age twelve to land allowing us the opportunity to bear arms and enjoy the other side of hunting for a change of venue.

Dad would bring home woodcock, grouse and pheasants two to three times a week leaving John and I with the cleaning chores when we came home from school, which we enjoyed knowing that we better get used to if we planned on joining the hunting fraternity in the near future. It was a year later that Dad thought we should learn to shoot rifles and shotguns which was awesome and then it dawned on us that we had more cleaning chores when we arrived back home, that being the art of stripping and cleaning guns.

You guessed it our chores were compounded, not only did we have game to dress but also added to the pile was cleaning Dad's guns as well. It was about 1947 when Dad was invited to hunt ducks with our dentist, Doc Koehler and that is when he dropped the upland game hunting to take up duck hunting.That led to a complete turn of events relative to equipment, boats, guns, change in clothing gear, boots, parkas, and decoys which he and his hunting buddies carved out of most any block of wood they could find. Decoys weighed a ton and were at best ugly and I wondered how stupid ducks were to fall for such relics.

They blew over in the water at a mere breath of wind and to counter that they attached wooden keels to the bottoms and poured lead into the bores in an effort to stabilize the decoys which only added more weight and as the decoys became water logged, they looked more like turtles on the water than ducks.

Decoys were put in army duffle bags acquired at the army surplus stores and at the end of the day we had to tote the bags down into the basement to thaw out for the next hunt. I am not certain where Dad got the decoy paint but when it got wet it feel in love with our clothes and bare skin and hung on like' tinner's red primer.

Drake Woodduck

Dad decided that it was time for me to learn the art of duck hunting at the ripe age of nine years old. He outfitted me with a pair of hip boots which at the time were just plain non insulated boots that were cold at forty degree temps and of course the ever loving red flannel long johns that hardly kept me warm in bed much less in frigid weather.

I remember piling on sweaters and a heavy jacket with a parka over that and by the time we reached the bay after the car heater running full blast for an hour I was sweating and that made for a frosty start once the cold air penetrated the sweat. I had chapped lips and a chapped ass before we hauled the bowling balls (decoys) to the blind. Dad was much better equipped as he became an L L Bean customer shortly after he experienced the elements that one had to deal with in quest of few ducks. He instructed me on how to unwind the decoy lines and carry the lead weights in one hand and the four foot decoy line in the other and gently set the decoy in the water to avoid tipping it over. When I entered the water I felt like I forgot to put my boots on due to the sweat inside my boots. To put this all into perspective in nineteen forty seven fish net underwear was not even on the radar screen nor were insulated boots, goretex and thinsulate and the winters were normally nasty along the great lakes every year.

We finished setting about fifty cement blocks (*decoys)* and I had to confirm that I still had two hands. When we finally got into the blind I shoved my hands down my pants to thaw and almost went into orbit when they touched my bare skin. At that point Dad asked me if wanted a sandwich and my lips were so damn cold I could not say yes or no.

Dad was a big eater and Mom would pack enough food to feed a hungry army. I could hardly swallow and he sat there packing them down like a chipmunk on a tree nut farm. I tried a banana and the damn thing stuck in my frozen throat and I thought it would take a plunger to extract the log jam.

His first words were sit very still and don't talk. If you see ducks whisper the clock hands for direction. 11–12–2. I already felt like a wooden Indian going to the outhouse and then he says don't move. I immediately thought when I get home I am going to tell Mom that Dad needs to visit a shrink. It wasn't long and few ducks flew into the ugliest decoys I had ever seen and Dad dropped one about twenty yards out in the water. He then said to me go get it before it drifts out of reach. That was when I realized hip boots only went up so far as I stepped about one foot too far and felt the nasty cold water filling my boots.

I wanted to scream but knew better, so I sucked it up and retrieved the duck and walked back to the blind hearing water slosh around in my boots. I told Dad I had to go behind the blind and relieve myself as an excuse to pull off my boots and empty the water out. I learned a very important lesson, do not take off your wet boots and try to pull them back on over wet wool socks as it is like trying to force a square peg in a round hole.

I hobbled around with my heels stuck up about five inches on the inside of my boots for about an hour until I managed to get my frozen feet back into the boots. As the day progressed I became too numb to feel much of anything keeping my hands close to my body until quitting time time which was more agony than I had anticipated. Each decoy had three foot lines attached to lead weights that had to be wound around the decoys one at a time.

The sand on the lines grated my frozen hands that were turning purple at the time. After bagging the decoys we each had to carry two swollen bags of decoys through sand for about four hundred yards to our car. When the heat finally kicked in my feet and hands were screaming when the circulation began to return to the surface ,however in spite of all the discomfort I managed to enjoy the day watching seagulls, shore birds and flocks of migrating ducks streaming into the eastern shore of Lake Erie to rest for the night. Whistling wings were endless as we picked up the decoys after shooting hours, which Dad abided to by to the minute.

Once home I headed for a tub of hot water which was a mistake as my frozen ass turned into a fireball and my feet when into scream mode as well. I remember looking at my butt in the mirror and cracked up thinking I looked like a zoo Baboon with the red cheeks glaring in the light. I will say that after a good hot meal and good nights sleep I felt I was hooked on waterfowl hunting for life and that has never changed.

I remember seeing about three blinds on Thompson Bay, which was my Dad's favorite duck hunting bay on Presque Isle Bay. There were a few scattered blinds along several miles of shore line that in later years became very crowded with blind about every three hundred feet totaling about three hundred plus blinds on several bays.

It was a duck hunting mecca for the hale and hearty to enjoy without the typical sky busting by rookies and or careless hunters. I would be entertained all day just watching all the birds that frequented the bay shores. Literally thousands of ducks would pass over during hard weather that seemed to chase them down from the nesting grounds up in northern Canada.

Little by little Dad improved my hunting gear and I eventually became immune to the discomforts of the cutting winds and cold temps on the bay and lake. He always said, it took a special breed to endure the harshness of the sport.

He took us to observe migrating flocks of ducks during the off seasons to observe migrating flocks that would fill the bays after gun season ended. He studied duck formations on the water to improve his decoy settings and he would quiz us on different species in flight and on the water, which enhanced our duck hunting in later years when certain duck species ended up on the protected list due to poor nesting seasons normally caused by droughts. Specie identity became big player as the hunting numbers increased over the years. It was more than a sport for Dad it was almost an obsession for him and over the years I analyzed his love for waterfowl hunting. It was easy once I pondered on it for sometime realizing that he lost his father when he was nine years old and pretty much had to fend for himself from that point on having to scrap and scratch to build a life for his family. Luxuries came hard for him and when he finally saw the light at the end of the tunnel he played hard to make up for many years of sacrifice. He loved his golf game as well but I think if he was put to the test he would say duck hunting ranked at the top of the deck. In retrospect I am happy that he found his passion and took full advantage of the best duck hunting to ever grace Lake Erie, perhaps never to be equalled due to overcrowding and inexperienced duck hunters. Dad passed away at the early age of sixty-one and the thought passed my mind at his grave site, that he was not deprived of several good years on earth, without a doubt but few that passed at his age could say those words.

Brother John and I became as close as two brothers could be due to our love for hunting a common ground that we will always cherish. Mom, John and I became very proficient at cleaning ducks as Dad managed to keep the larders full and Mom was an excellent wild game cook ,therefore our game never went unappreciated. Dad slowly equipped us with proper gear, as good as it was at the time ,and as we approached hunting age he readied us with proper gun training stressing the importance of gun safety.

New decoys were hitting the market, Herters, Majestic and L L Bean to mention a few and that's when Dad ordered three dozen Majestic decoys and trashed his closet full of enamored wooden boat anchors that had served their time and purpose. Majestic decoys were the state of the art at the time and cost sixty dollars a dozen. They were tough vinyl/plastic mallard decoys and relatively good sized with built in keels that were impossible to roll over even in rough waters, which was a selling point with Dad after fighting the roll over ratio with home made woods.

Dad lost his hunting partner Doc Koehler at a young age and began hunting with one of his work associates. Louie Diehl and I would say at the very least they hunted three to four days a week, bearing in mind the seasons back then were of much shorter durations so they had to double up on the good hunting days. Louie did not eat duck so we ended up cleaning two limits most every evening, the limit at the time was four ducks per hunter without the specie restrictions that followed in ensuing years as management became more scientific and Ducks Unlimited became major players in setting bag limits based on their data collection capabilities. Louie built a sturdy row boat to help set the decoys and retrieve them at the end of the day which improved the water soaked boot syndrome immensely.

It was not unusual to set decoys in the morning only to have the water level rise one to two feet due to wind direction changes thus making the pick up chores ending up with filled boots to drive home in to end the day. Many times we would have to toss weighted lines out to snag decoy lines to avoid going two feet above our hip boots.

Being a couple of years older than John I was the first to bear arms in the duck blind. Speaking of blinds, Dad had the same blind for fifteen years and we never had to take it down as it was across the bay in a weeded area pretty much out of sight. It later became blind number eighteen at Thompson Bay, once blind drawings became the norm to avoid all of the hassles for the good of the order.

My first shotgun was a Remington model 31 twenty gauge pump with a twenty- six inch barrel. Many laughed and said it was a good upland game gun but paled in comparison to a good Winchester twelve gauge three inch magnum for waterfowl hunting, which is what Dad used for years.

Ironically I passed both guns down to our son Scott a few years ago and they are still in mint condition seventy plus years later, and when I say they had a ton of use that is an understatement. Dad laid the law down up front with no wiggle room, one shell only the first year. His reasoning was two fold, first it only takes one well placed shot to drop a duck within thirty yards and number two he did not want the excitement to cause an accident by having more rounds in the magazine.

I observed other hunters on the bay that would inadvertently empty their guns after missing the first and best shot and in most cases the ducks were out of range for the last two rounds.
Just busting holes in the sky as Dad would say. I was well prepared with ammo as our uncle Walter was a colonel in the army and he gave us several fifty caliber machine gun ammo boxes that were perfect to tote shells and we always had a full

box and seldom came home with any live shells and at best maybe one duck that was racked up as a lucky shot.
Bear in mind sky busting was not acceptable with Dad so point made all shots were pigeon shots as we later referred to easy shots. It took some time and many shots but eventually I began to connect fairly regularly. My second season was much better after I learned how to swing and follow through.

In later years hunting the same bays with friends that got into duck hunting later in life they would look at me like I was loco when I told them about the way it was growing up with Dad and John. We would be sitting in a blind for hours and never see a duck and at best may have three to four shots all day and thats when I broke out the old stories from past seasons and they would find it hard to believe until, another old timer would stop and chat and reinforce what I,was saying. Sad but true there were and still are good duck numbers and my guess is they are better today than they were back in the forties and fifties.

The big difference today is there is much more gun pressure and the ducks are a lot smarter. The best part of the day was just before first light when we were setting decoys hearing wing beats over head in the darkness. If that did not get your engine going nothing would. I always said when the heartbeat remains constant at first light it is time to stay in bed and sell your gear.

John joined the party a couple of years later and it wasn't long before we had Dad and others looking differently at our twenty gauge shotguns. John used a Winchester twenty gauge with a twenty-six inch barrel. Dad soon converted to a twenty gauge as well and found he did better as it was less weight to swing and you were forced to draw down a bit tighter.
The killing power was there just less pattern to work with thus it made a better gunner out of the shooter. Federal came out with a two and three quarter number six shot magnum loads that really improved our knock down power. Each year saw more newcomers to the sport but very few made the hard weather

teams that reaped the harvest when the bigger hard weather ducks arrived like the Canvasbacks and Red Heads.
I will never forget one day in December we were hit with a weather front from hell. It cleared in the afternoon and I was hunkered down in a bull rushes staying warm when I heard geese, and tons of them overhead. I crawled out of the comfort and the sky was black with Canada's, Blue's and Snows and I could not believe my eyes. As a youngster I had never seen wild geese and believed that I never would. They were a tad long for my twenty gauge and I did not want to risk a body shot so I just hunkered down and took in the show.

Redheads

Today we have Canada's all over the country thanks to DU and other wildlife efforts to restore the beautiful geese. Dad managed to drop a Snow goose and it blew my mind it as it was so big compared to our ducks and John and I had the pleasure, or should I say the nasty job of cleaning the Snow and when we drew the innards the smell was off the charts and had us both gagging in the process.

We dry plucked all of our ducks and dipped them in hot paraffin wax and let them cool and then peeled the down off with ease. Some just cut out the breast to avoid all the hassle but we liked to stuff the cavity with cooking onions to draw the strong taste out making for excellent table fare.
John and I worked for Dad during our summer vacations and most of our earnings went to shotgun shells as we enjoyed hand thrown skeet shooting and we always caught the spring crow migrations that followed the lake shore and it was a good warm

up for duck season as well.

Dad invested in a fancy LL Bean duck boat that he truly treasured and we were able to mount a light three horse power Evinrude motor to make setting and collecting decoy chores a more livable. Dad had been having trouble with his model twelve three inch magnum discharging unexpectedly when he chambered a three inch shell. It only happened on a few occasions but it did it always scared the hell out of him and anyone nearby. He visited our gun smith on two occasions and was told it was a fluke and must have been a bad round.

We were all hunting in the same blind one day and Dad dropped a Red Head and it dove and headed out into the bay and Dad hopped into his trusty Bean boat and chased the duck down only to have the duck shed the first two high base shells off like water. Frustrated he stood up in the boat and decided to try a three inch shell and as he rammed the chamber shut the round went off and punched a large hole in the bottom of the boat. In desperation he pulled out his red hunting hanky and tried to plug the hole, which at the time looked like a whale clearing his blow hole. John and I were on the shore busting a gut as Dad rowed his torpedo ridden baby to shore and the first thing out of his mouth was, don't tell your Mother what happened. Right Dad! How can we not share the funniest thing in the world with everyone we know? John and had a race to the back door to tell Mom who was laughing hysterically when Dad walked in the door and it did not take him long to figure out that one of his sons and hunting buddies spilled the beans and of course we both denied being the one that told Mom. We had fun with that story for years to come and still enjoy telling it to hunting friends. On a similar note, as long as I am roasting Dad, one night we rowed across Thompson Bay to unload and lock up the boat in the dark after shooting hours. John and I were always relegated to row the boat as Dad navigated from the rear of the boat yelling hard right of hard left adjusting to wind issues as he guided us to the spot on the beach that was closest to our tree where we unloaded and secured the boat. We happened to be in our heavy row boat and when John I stepped out we always grabbed the bow and gave it a hard tug to beach the boat on the sand. This particular night when we gave the customary heave ho we heard a big splash only to find out that Dad had been standing on the back seat getting ready to step out when we tugged and was now laying on his back in two feet of freezing water spouting like a sperm whale. My first thought was where is his gun? John and I about chewed our lower lips off to avoid losing control and getting a boat oar across our heads.

The hundred yard path to the truck was a long miserable walk for Dad. John walked ahead and I brought up the rear and to watch Dad walk with five gallons of water in his boots and pants was a sight to behold. Kind of like a giant penguin and or a man with loaded britches. Dad never struck us growing up but I had a feeling that may change if I tripped his trigger with one of my normal wise cracks at such opportune times.

John is more like my Dad, fairly reserved and I got my Mom's funny bone which at times was hard to conceal and believe me this was one of those Kodak moments that sent me over the top. It was a solemn ride home. and when Dad walked in the door drenched Mom busted a gut, however Dad found but little humor in it for several months. On another memorable day we had a nasty wind change to the northwest and it came in quick and hard and Dad opted to pull up the set and move to the north end of Thompson Bay for better wind advantage and a break from the cutting wind.

Dad and I were in a row boat loaded with decoys and I was on the oars and finding the wind more than a little challenging, with the bay kicking up some serious white caps and straining the oars to beat hell and after Dad took on a few puss full's of splash from the oars he barked at me to bury the oars for more bite at which time I lost my cool and stood up and put all the muscle I could muster and let it rip and bingo both oars snapped in half and the paddle ends went flying off in the wake. Thompson bay was separated from the east end of Lake Erie by a sandbar that was not all that wide and we were spinning at the mercy of the high winds and fast moving white caps headed for the lake that was heaving with sizable white caps as well.

My first thought was, where the hell is a submarine when you need one? It was a crap shoot, do we bail and try to make it to shore or do we play roulette and hope the sandbar beaches the boat. It was not a good father and son moment but we lucked out and caught the tip of the sandbar and were able to get our boots on the beach and haul the boat and decoys up on the sandbar for a breather. I was elected to walk the boat around the bay to the north end of the bay and once again was soaked in the process.

It was yet another quiet ride home again that became a laughing matter a few weeks down the road. Lake Erie is the shallowest lake of the Great Lakes and we had many occasions to test our steel out fishing and duck hunting on numerous occasions and it goes without saying that it can and will get your attention at times. We respected her rage and always had our senses tuned in but she still managed to catch us with our pants down on several occasions, although we never lost our cool no matter how dire the situation was and over the years we had to deal with some nasty weather conditions that went along with the territory.

I can count on one hand the days that I came home dry and even close to being warm but I relished every moment of my time with Dad and John sitting in duck blinds. Ducks wore wrist watches and knew when the day ended and they would swarm up the east lake to the bay and we never missed sitting on our chained boat and taking in the spectacle at the close of the day. As the years progressed those sights diminished and I am not certain what changed to take those incredible moments away. It was a great way to end the day and remind us of the reason we were hooked on water fowling. We used to ask each other when the going got rough at times,would you do this for a living? That always eased the tensions and discomforts and collected comments that we should have logged for future posterity. Dad always said, if you want to find out what a man is made of take him hunting. I never forgot those word and over the years discovered that he was right on the money.

We lived within a mile of the main bay and we could hear the guns going off when we were dressing for school and it drove us to distraction at times. Our school was also close to the bay and when we recessed outside our ears were tuned in to bay listening for shots. Every year around Christmas break most of my the teachers would place their orders for ducks, venison or birds and Mom would drive me to school and I would pass out the game. It was kind of an appeasement for the days we called in sick and when I would hand my teachers my admit slip after being out sick they would grin and say things like, home is the hunter home from hill or welcome back nimrod, knowing where we were on stormy days.

I would not trade my boyhood for a full ride to Harvard due to the memories and experiences that far surpass any book learning that may have been missed due to hunting time with my Dad and John. We both went on to college and have done well in life so there is no regrets in the memory banks. Life is much different today in the fast lanes and I doubt that it is even close to getting better. Life was at a much slower pace in the forties and early fifties. John and I both played sports but unlike today when the seasons were over we had plenty of time to enjoy doing many other things of interest, like hunting and fishing or target shooting. Today kids in sports are compelled to train twenty-four sevens all year and seldom have a day to pursue other interests as a result the hunting fraternity is suffering for lack of new comers to the outdoor life. Our entire family of uncles and cousins were all avid outdoorsmen and believe it or not we all have done quite well without the twenty-four seven sports dictating how we spend every waking hour of our life. Young boys could not wait to buy a hunting license and get into the outdoors. We all started with our Daisey BB guns and make believe safari hunts in nearby woodlots.

Dad was always good about letting us bring a buddy out with us to get taste of duck and deer hunting. He bought a used Willys station wagon and to say we got great use out of it would be an understatement. We would get up early on school days and drive out to the head of the peninsula where there was a marshy area and hunt for one half hour and then beat feet for school leaving guns and ammo and decoys in the Jeep, unlike today where we would have been collared and taken to jail.
Matter of fact there were occasions that I would carry a shotgun into a teachers office to show him what I used. Several teachers hunted and enjoyed talking guns and hunting stories. When I turned twelve I would walk five miles to our crow blinds west of town out of the city limits in the spring walking through high end neighborhoods carrying my shotgun and a pack full of shells and quite often one of our city policemen would pick me up and drop me off near the woodlot that we hunted in not far from home.

We had several duck blinds built that we were able to leave up all year and just clean up and paint every duck hunting season. Wind direction and weather would predicate where we would set up for the day With minimal gun pressure the duck hunting was as good as it gets. The only challenge at the time was a section of the peninsula road would get flooded at times preventing us from getting to the blinds on Thompson and Misery Bays. On occasion we would cross the big bay in outboards in predawn hours and land north of the washed out road and where Dad had permission to park one of his contracting company pick up trucks well north of the road closure area.

We would beach the boat and transfer decoys and one row boat to the truck and then off we would go for the day not knowing if we would have to cross the bay again in the dark or drive the pick up home. Was the shooting good on those days? Off the charts wonderful, and we normally bagged out early and would just sit in the blinds watching thousands of duck heading south out of Canada. On a couple of occasions Dad and a few other hunters were forced to hang out at the Coast Guard Station over night until the road became passable the next day. It was several years later that the Army Corps of Engineers was summoned to deal with the ever eroding road issues. Today no one would ever guess that Erie was very close to losing the rare peninsula that attracts visitors to the beaches every year.

Jackie and I have lived in Colorado for twenty three years, sad but true I have not returned to my native state since leaving, however some of my fondest memories are of duck hunting on Lake Erie and they remain as fresh and vivid as if only happening yesterday. John and I often talk about the good old days when only a handful of duck hunters frequented our stomping grounds and I am certain many still enjoy the bay hunting but rest assured there will never be a time for duck hunting like the forties and fifties. We seldom came home with dry boots as in the course of the day we all managed to step in a hole and fill one or both boots and it always happened at predawn setting decoys which would make for long day.

We had a few standard initiations for our friends that asked to come along and try duck hunting. When they would step in over their boots we would tell them to lay on their backs and lift their legs straight up in the air and when the icy water ran up their ass they knew they had been the victim of a prank and then would wait for our newbie to step behind the blind to relieve himself then we would remove the chambered shell and replace it with one that we had loaded without shot leaving primer, powder and wad and after he would step back in the blind we would wait until a nice flock of ducks would set in and tell the him it was his turn to shoot first and when he pulled the trigger fire and smoke would fill the air when the dud went off. It never failed to be a crowd pleaser. We always cleared the barrel before reloading to be certain we did not harm the gun.

Another favorite was to wait until the our new hunter was biting into a sandwich then we would jump up and aim our guns like there were ducks over the decoys. Invariably they would drop their sandwich in the sand and raise their gun to shoot and when they retrieved their sandwich the first bite was a nasty sandy coated gritty bite. We always had plenty of food so they did not starve. We had similar newbie stunts for the deer camp and ice fishing in winter.

Hunting was so fraternal back then that most hunters left decoys in bags behind their blinds in fifty gallon drums until their next hunt. Dad bought livery boats that needed some repairs and John and I had fun replacing rotten transoms and oar locks and painting them olive drab of light grey. We could load two on the jeep at a time and we used them for both duck hunting and fishing. There was never a season of the year that we were not doing something to better our equipment to improve our duck hunting seasons.

Early on once I became fairly tuned into duck hunting Dad would occasionally drop me off with the decoys and head back to his office to take care of some business matters and be back in time for the late afternoon hunt. We seldom if ever encountered federal game wardens until later years when the hunter numbers increased. On one occasion I was set up on Misery Bay near the channel going into Horseshoe Pond that was a protected area due to a large number of house boats.I knocked down a Bluebill and let it drift into a small inlet where I could retrieve it with ease, or so I thought. I walked along a steel reinforcement retaining wall which was about three feet high and it appeared my duck was washed up on the sand and I jumped off the bank and bingo, I was sucked into sand up to my waist in a nano second. As luck would have it there was a three quarter by two foot rebar sticking out of the steel wall allowing me to grab hold of something substantial enough to manage to pull myself slowly back onto the wall. It was a cold wet day and I was soaked to my skin all over and my hip boots were loaded with water and sand. There was little or no traffic which was typical of the Peninsula on dreary bitter days and I knew I had to get out of my clothes and try to dry out so I gathered drift wood and was able to start a fire with matches that I had wrapped in foil for such occasions. I could not take my boots off due to heavy wet socks binding the boots too tight to budge.I was collecting good heat from the hot fire and was able to at least dry my long john tops and sweater and hunting jacket. Just when I felt half way human the water in my books began to boil and burn the hell out of my legs. I cut the sides of both boots with my knife to relieve the burn knowing it was better to have to deal with buying new hips than scalding my legs.

Dad showed up about four hours later and I opted to tough it out and tell him after quitting time to avoid ruining his time to hunt. He always had plenty of chow and hot chocolate and that helped handle a few more hours of hunting that day. Duck hunting was not for wimps and we all came to accept that there would be days that we had to suck it up so the rest of our hunting party could enjoy a full day of hunting. As the years progressed major equipment improvements began to surface and helped with the weather discomforts to some extent. I used to say the person that can design a pair of waders with a zipper fly in lieu of having to get half undressed to take a leak will become an instant millionaire.

We used pump guns due to the blowing and wet sand that would bugger up the auto loaders and it took a gun smith to take them apart and clean ,whereas we could field strip our pumps in minutes to clean out the sand.

Our day was not over when we landed at the truck. Once home we would drag the decoys down into the basement to thaw out and check the anchor lines and let the sand dry off so they would be ready for the next hunt. Guns were attended to almost immediately along with parkas,boots,waders and of course our bag of the day had to be cleaned and made freezer ready.
We always soaked our ducks after cleaning in cold salt water to draw out the blood to eliminate the strong taste that some

species (*primarily the diver species)*, dipper ducks, mallards, teal, baldpate. woodies, and pintails were always better table fare for our money.

There were always surprises every season and adjustments were always in order almost on a daily basis. I remember Dad walking in the house with the biggest duck that we had never seen. It appeared to be a very large Bluebill (greater scaup)but much larger, although it had the same head and body shape and matching colors of the Bluebill but it was almost three times the size of the Lesser Scaup. Ironically a month later Field and Stream featured a story called, Nordern Bluebills, (*not northern)* and the pictures were exactly what Dad had brought home.
We never did identify other Nordern's during our hunts and we figured it was a fluke. sOn another occasions Dad came home with a Black Duck that was the size of a Blue Goose. It had been banded in Nova Scotia and according to the report mailed back it was eleven years old.

One day on our way to the bay we were hit with a blinding snow storm and we lost the road and had to break out the compass to orient, and one hunter walked the road feeling for

the edge to make certain we did not drive thru a car wash on the way to our blind. Once we were able to take the road that angled east we were out of the blizzard and managed to locate the parking lot at Thompson Bay. I remember setting decoys and a flock of over hundred Bufflehead landed in the decoys and I could have picked up my limit by hand.
They were swimming all around me and made for a great moment. As the snow subsided and daylight hit, our decoys were loaded with ducks and of all things several Surf Scoters which blew our minds. We just sat there and absorbed the moment and eventually they swam out into the middle to the bay. We never shot at ducks on the water and we had no desire to shoot Surf Scoters that were not good table fare, but the moment lingered for years as we seldom saw Scoters in the years that followed.
We always enjoyed inviting high school chums to tag along on our hunts and one of my high school buddies. Dick Foran loved to duck hunt and one day he shot his first duck, an American Merganser and it took me a couple of hours to settle him down. He had the duck in his lap for most of the day and never took his eyes off of it all the way home. I told him that it was a fish duck and not the best table fare but he did not care and was anxious to show his Mom. A week later he told me that his Mom made him remove the duck from the fire place mantle in the living room because it was getting smelly. That story made the rounds for several years. Hunting stories never get old and the more they are hashed over the more enjoyable they become some more priceless than others but they all made the books. We were blessed to have had the great experiences that Dad provided for us and he never balked at our bringing a friend along that otherwise never would have had the opportunity to enjoy a day duck hunting. In later years I enjoyed duck hunting with three of my nephews Paul and Terry Pfeffer, Scott Woodworth and our son Scott. I will elaborate on those wonderful years in my next book,"Buck Beach and Field Commander."

In the early fifties Dad took John and I to Matamuskeet North Carolina. to hunt a regulated waterfowl hunting area that was awesome. At the time John and I had never bagged a goose but that was soon to change.

Drake Pintail

We landed late at night and the geese flying over the lodge had us wound up to a point that we could not sleep. They conducted blind drawings every night and then our guide met us at the lodge in morning to take us out to our designated blind for the day's hunt. Our guide appeared to be hung over and was not a friendly sort but that did not dampen our spirits. We had a long hump through typical swamp muck and when we landed at the blind we noticed the decoys were left out permanently and were just tossed out in random fashion. This was not the way we had perceived the first day would be but we were patient and opted to let the day play out. Our non social guide sat behind the blind sunning himself and moaning that the weather was too warm and the ducks and geese would hang out on protected waters all day and lift off at night and we were wasting our time.

We could hear thousands of ducks and geese talking on the reservoir and ignored the guide and it paid off and within an hour before quitting time the sky was blacked out with ducks and geese at optimum range and within fifteen minutes we all had our limits of ducks and geese and our sorry ass guide was scrambling all over the bullrushes gathering our birds which made our day. We dropped our game off at a small farm house for cleaning and freezing for our return trip home.

Dad registered a complaint at the lodge about our lethargic guide and they set us up for a field hunt the next day and it was a day to remember. We were all set in separate blinds about one hundred yards apart and at the crack of dawn a flock of Canada's started to circle our decoys and my heart was pounding so hard I could hardly hear the geese chatter as they made their second and third sweep of the three separate set ups. I was praying that they would set into Dad or John to kick things off but as luck would have it they made a bee line for my set up and I was not certain when to stand up and start the fire works.

When I did make my move I was awestruck at the sight of so many geese in my face. I emptied out and saw one lazy feather floating down to the cut corn and stood their in disbelief.
By then John and I were very good shots on ducks and to believe I never touched a large goose was embarrassing and hard to fantasize. The flock flared over Dad and he dropped one between the blinds and I hightailed it out to retrieve his prize and hold a goose for the first time in my hunting career.

We were all in Dad's blind reveling at the experience when we heard circling honkers and we all hit the floor on our knees peeking through the corn stalks stacked against the wire on the front of the blind. Sure enough we had an even larger flock heading straight for our set up. Dad was always prone to charley horses in his muscular legs and bingo one hit him and he went down groaning as the flock set in and John and I opened up and when the birds were counted we had five on the ground.
Dad said he never fired a shot which meant one of us had tripled on geese. Later that evening in the lodge dining room we were sitting next to two federal wardens and when they asked Dad how the hunt went and popping his buttons, Dad told them that one of his boys actually tripled on geese that morning. The wardens grinned and said you do know the bag limit is two geese per hunter. Dad looked like the guy that just pooped the bed, he did not have much to say. The warden enjoyed the moment and left it at that. Dad talked about that incident for many years to come.

One of his favorite expressions was even a fish can get in trouble if he opens his mouth enough. Naturally I was smart enough to avoid repeating his teachings. We hunted five days and bagged out on ducks and geese everyday and when we stopped my the cleaning house to pick up our birds we were told that we had twenty-five birds over the possession limit for crossing state lines. Dad thought we would not have any problems as everything was in boxes.

Leaving town Dad said we best find a gas station to fill up as it was getting late and we were in the country and gas stations were few and far between, We finally found a single pump gas station that was open and as we drove up the sign on the wall said, gas and state game warden. The warden came out to pump gas and Dad was out of the car engaging the warden by chatting about everything but hunting. John and I were certain we would get busted but Dad managed to dodge another bullet and get us down the road out of the Carolinas. In retrospect we had a great time but we all agreed it was way too easy a hunt and we never returned.

We mixed in swamp,pond and creek floats primarily during the early seasons to warm our barrels waiting for the hard weather to drive the ducks down from Canada and also drive the fair weather hunters off the bay to eliminate the frustration from sky busting and hunters wearing the orange field hunting garb. Collecting good numbers was never a problem due to Dad's scientific approach to setting decoys and drawing most ducks that entered the bay to our set ups. He was a task master when it came to doing what was necessary to pull the birds in regardless of wind conditions. We sometimes reset the decoys every hour with wind changes dictating that if we wanted to be successful we would endure all conditions. The very worst case scenario was when we had cold rains turning to snow snd the snow sticking to the decoys making them look like mounds of snow on the water.

Dad would say ok boys we have to go and dunk each decoy to get rid of the snow or flat out go home as we will not attract ducks to turtles. Cold does not describe the effort even close. Our hands would be so numb it was hard to handle a gun for long periods of time until we managed to thaw them out. Gloves were a joke then and still remain so today. Dad got the bright idea that we should rub glycerine on the decoys to prevent the ice from sticking to them and it did work for a while but did not prove to be worth the effort. We tried wearing muskrat trapping gloves that were rubberized with sleeves that came well above our elbows. They worked well in warmer weather but were cumbersome and created more work than good. Then came the handy hand warmers that created more burns than heat so we scraped that program as well. They were about as useless as battery operated socks which proved to be yet another farce.

Each year we encountered new hunters and early on they were true die in the wool duck hunters and we seldom had any issues with sky busting at ducks well out of range and not allowing ducks that would have decoyed to finish their swings and passes. Like most things in life we just accepted the change in ethics and lived on past memories to pacify the changes that were encroaching on our beloved sport. We were constantly trying new ways to speed up the setting up and taking down our decoys and after much trial and error we found the best method was to attach two inch plastic rings to a master line made from quarter inch nylon cord which we dyed a dark color to blend in with the water. We tied the rings to master cord every three feet and attached two foot lines with snaps on about a dozen decoys and then we made anchors out of one pound coffee cans by filling cans with concrete and setting u shaped wire into the mix to set up and be used to anchor both ends of the master lines thus allowing us to set a dozen decoys at a time and being able to reset them quickly by using a gaff hook to fish out the lead anchor without freezing out hands off.

We would lay out the master lines on the shore and attach decoys and then set the lead anchor in the row boat and drag the decoys out and the drop the anchor to position the decoys with the wind perfectly. We left about two dozen decoys loose with long lines to use as filler between the master lines. Pick up was fast and easy and we would reverse the system to collect and bag the decoys on shore without being hassled with wind and darkness. Ducks followed the lead line decoys perfectly and offered a field of fire conducive to safe and accurate shooting lanes. Not only did the new idea make for faster set ups and ease of overall task management but it improved our bag limits as well. Every year the bay became more crowded and hunters became less patient with the what and where they could build blinds. Some were too close for safety and many were basic hodgepodge looking non functional shacks that blew apart in the first wind and cluttered the bays after the hunting seasons.

Peninsula police chief at the time, Carl Rosanske tired of all the bickering laid down the law creating a first come first serve drawing for blind sites and staked where they would be permitted to be erected. This created a push come to shove situation and it appeared we may be losing our duck hunting rights on the bay for good. There were the usual cheats and smart alecks to deal with on draw day that added to the irritation for the chief and without the help of a few dedicated duck hunters led by Jack Vantassel, Jerry Honnard, and Jerry Klein and a few others forming the NorthWest Pa Duck Hunters Association. there is little doubt in my mind that the chief would have ended the duck hunting on Prequel Isle Bay. It took a few years for the new order to settle in and all would except the way things would be in a very fair and equitable way. It then became a drawing and the hunters that were lucky enough to get a blind in the drawing were notified and a date was set for them to draw according to number they drew. It was very fair and well conducted event and most had but little reason to complain and to the best of my knowledge that is still the procedure today. It goes without saying that the founding fathers of the North West Duck Hunters Association, saved the right to hunt ducks on Presque Isle Bay and to this day the organization still prevails and is dong a yeoman's task at preserving the right to hunt on the Isle. My hat is off to such dedication by so few for so many.

Every duck hunter in or near Erie Pa needs to cut a check and get involved is this commendable organization. Hunters and fisherman alike fail to be supportive of the organizations that keep their chosen sports alive and well and need to jump in and offer time, money or both if you hope to preserve the rights for generations to follow.While you are at it join Ducks Unlimited

the Big Daddy of them all when it comes to waterfowl. Rest assured becoming apart of Northwest Duck Hunter will make you a more complete and more ethical duck hunter. They are a full plate with a plethora of activities for all ages to enjoy and acquire better duck hunting skills.

Do it todayBefore you Forget

Chapter Two:
Sink Boxes and Power Boats

Once John and I were experienced guns and the hunt Dad opted to get into the latest rage of duck hunting with sink boxes or float boxes as some referred to them. If you wanted a box you had to build your own and that was not exactly an easy task due to the fact that there was no blueprints at the time and many deemed the thought to be a cut below a kamikaze suicide pilots.

For those that do not know what a sink box is allow me to give you a brief description to the best of my recollection. A box is about ten feet long and five feet wide with the front and sides tapering down from the cockpit to the water creating a seamless look where the water and the box met. The cockpit, was designed to allow the gunner to step into the box from the service boat, which was normally an eighteen foot outboard open deck design. The back that was anchored against the wind was hollowed out to counter incoming waves preventing them from soaking the unsuspecting gunner. The box was constructed using three quarter inch marine plywood floor and quarter inch sidewalls and then coated with fiberglass to seal the joints and stiffen the overall structure.

Louie Diehl was the master boat builder in the group and designed and built different designs all of which stood the test of time. Once the box was built and fiberglassed the next major task was to choose the perfect shade of grey that would blend in with the water in different weather and light conditions. Cloudy overcast days was not a problem, however when the sun popped out between the clouds the light grey would brighten considerably illuminating the box. We settled on a box for the early season that tended to have more sunshine and one for the later season that would blend with the dark better adapted to the sunny days than on gloomy days. The anchor system was simple yet it had to be reinforced as the box was anchored at both the front and rear ends to keep the it from swinging right to left in the wind much like a kite tied to one end only. Waves varied and the rear anchor had to be fortified much more than the front.The inside of the box had a sloped back panel and ample leg room for the gunner to stretch out and slide his torso down almost to a reclined position thus keeping his head and eyes just peeking over the front of the cockpit. Bear in mind ducks are approaching the decoys from many to sometime hundreds of feet above the water and there are many eyes on the set up looking for safe a landing zone. Hunters wore grey hoodies to blend with the box as opposed to dark colors that would clash and flare the approaching ducks. Ready set wait a minute. How are we going to tow the box or boxes out into they waters in predawn light with about one hundred decoys as opposed to a few bags for shore blind hunting?

Box hunting was kind of like a new suit and now you need new shoes and ties to complete the outfit. We had Louie's home made flat bottom run about which was sufficient for the shore hunts but bear in mind we will have a hunter two to three hundred yards off shore with no means to row or navigate the box in a mayday situation and they were frequent flyers on Lake Erie. Winds would go from gentle to flat out nasty in a matter of minutes. We picked up a used wolverine eighteen foot outboard that was plenty sea worthy with a ten horse mercury which was adequate and dependable. We had to slide in close and grab the box to drop off and pickup hunters allowing them to step out of the box with full gear which included a shell vest, hip boots,parka and gun and the water was quite rough at times. Some hunters that attempted the task with lesser equipment either drowned or came close, sending a strong message, that being, do it right or stay on the shore. We alternated hunters every hour or if it was slow day we might extend the time.

It was a bit confining and with only a three quarters of an inch of lumber between your butt and the water it was about the limit to insure the hunter was nimble enough to make the transition from box to boat. When the gunner had a bird down and identified as wounded or dead we had red flags that he would signal to the pick up boat on the beach. Pickup man or men would chase down at the wounded duck and kill the motor before finishing off the bird and then collect with a large fish net to avoid getting a bath in the process.

We had several options when we first started setting boxes and there was only about three box hunters on the entire bay at the time. Dad checked his barometer twice a day and was excellent at wind direction and speed estimates and when we hit the bay we knew where the ducks would be coming into with wind and weather conditions. Occasionally we bet wrong and had to drag up and reset into quieter water. We always liked to be on the lee side and in from where the wind and water began to wave up for safety and also to prevent the gunner from having to shoot off a bucking bronco in rough water.

It was a new world for us and many adjustments had to be made to debug the program. Decoy lines had to be thirty feet long with added weights to prevent the set from blowing apart. Wind shifts would change set ups and gunner had to signal the shore team to come out and reset some or all of the decoys. We liked to create a horseshoe layout forcing the incoming ducks to align on the gunner offering maximum range of movement.

Judging range in a semi prone position was a problem initially due to the line of sight was from the front edge of the cockpit to several feet beyond the inside to the set. We would inadvertently come up way too soon and flare the ducks well out of range.We discovered the best rule of thumb was to wait until we clearly spotted the feet of the lead birds and that solved the problem. Coming up from a semi prone position as opposed to two feet on the ground was yet another adjustment.

Swing and follow though was off as was the gun stock fitting into a cramped position often requiring shorter stocks to compensate for the loss of mobility. We typically liked four hunters on board to create a viable work crew to function properly and safely. Set up time was always a fun time as we towed the box behind our outboard with decoy bags piled high in the bow area. First step was to set the box and anchor fore and aft being certain that we had the back anchor firmly set and then stretching out the front anchor and setting the front of the box

Once the box was set we would begin digging into the decoy bags and one at a time unwind thirty foot decoy lines and set them three foot apart. This entire operation was done an hour before shooting hours and our only light was from the city lights from the harbor area and of course flash lights that for the most part was a waste of time. We would set over one hundred decoys and if the wind was up it only compounded the effort and keeping the boat and prop away from the set decoys could at times become annoying. Team work was the order of the day and we let the boat drift away from the box as we set the decoys. In a perfect day we were set up about fifteen minutes from legal shooting time with first gunner set and ready.

We had to work fast and accurately to avoid major headaches and it was seldom a smooth ride but we always felt it was worth the effort. Later on the bay became over crowded with boxes and it was difficult to find a good spot to set boxes. Once the box was set and gunner in place we headed for shore and normally had a beach set up as well so those waiting their turn in the box had a chance at some shore shooting. One hunter was assigned the task of keeping a close eye on the box both for downed ducks and or sudden wind or weather changes that required us to run out and reset the decoys and reposition the box for the best shooting angle and also hunter safety from being broadsided by waves. It was a rare day that we did not limit out but we did have a few of those all work and no ducks to show for our efforts.

Most of our ducks taken from the boxes were of the diver class, red heads,bluebills, ring neck ducks,golden eyes,canvasbacks butterballs (buffleheads) and occasionally we lucked out with a few mallards and blacks.

Lake Erie was notorious for wind and weather changes and without much warning, consequently you had to keep you game face on when working the boxes. When we were hit off guard the first concern was to get the gunner out of the box and then secure the box and worry about collecting the decoys.

There were times when heavy snow would blind us from seeing the box and that was unnerving at best. I was trapped in a box on Misery Bay one day for over two hours in a blinding snowstorm and Dad and John could not risk running the boat into the box looking for me. I hunkered down and covered the hatch with a tarp to try and stay warm and your imagination can run rampant in such situations. You think you hear outboard motors and even big power boats and you remove as much clothing as possible just in case you have to hit the water and swim with the life jacket in bitter cold water and air temps. The storm finally lifted and Dad and John pulled me out of the box and when I hit shore my feet were screaming with pain. I pulled my boots off and put my bare feet in the bay water to cut the pain in both feet and hands. Collecting the decoys and loading the boat and box was a bit of an ordeal but we normally talked about where we would set up the next day.

Duck hunting was not for the faint of heart but for those that walked the line it was worth the effort and sometimes pain and the memories are priceless. Once we became proficient with the box hunting we opted to add a second box to the set up allowing two gunners at a time by setting the boxes about forty feet apart and in line with one another. This allowed us to accommodate more hunters and we felt it would be safer and more enjoyable for all the gunners. The trick was to designate a field of fire for both boxes. It had the added advantage of capitalizing on the hot hours when the ducks were active allowing us to fill out sooner and being able to collect decoys and boxes in better light and weather conditions as opposed to doing all of the pick ups near of after dark. I remember well on given days we would have two hundred to three hundred ducks at a time dive down from high altitudes into our set up and when they poured into the decoys at max speed offering some tricky shots from all angles. Mud Hens (coots) were fun for the beginning hunters to warm their barrels on and that is a good place to start.

At the time the limit on mud hens was twenty-five per day, however we seldom wasted ammo on a bird that was not good table fare and we did not shoot and leave birds as many did on a regular basis. Like all things better decoys became available and one local artisan, Jack Sweet produced the best oversized wooden decoys on the planet and later produced styrofoam decoys in many species and they were state of the art as well incorporating dual wells on the bottoms to act as suction cups keeping the decoys right side in foul weather and high winds.

My brother in law, the late Mel Pfeffer, owned a pattern shop and had all of the equipment including kilns and was able to mold his own styrofoam decoys as did a few others and they saved a lot of decoy money over the years. Mel and my two nephews Terry and Paul were avid duck hunters and we shared many hours in the blinds in the later years.

We had Portuguese cork oversized mallards that were state of the art as well although the new breed of decoys were awesome they did not take the abuse the old clunkers took and therefore we had to handle more carefully. Competition on the shore blinds became a real problem at times due to sky busting and hunters showing up to set decoys right at prime time scaring off ducks that would have set into somebody's set. Dad became a bit disgruntled and thought we should find a bigger boat to handle lake hunting east of Erie near twenty mile creek closer to

Northeast Pa. Dad and our neighbor George Graham set out to find an old inboard that needed work and was priced right. After months of searching they pulled into our driveway with a boat that I am certain survived the battle of Lake Erie and I was it must have been in Admiral Perry's fleet as a decoy for the British cannons

At any rate we had out work cut out for us and it took several months to cut out the dry rot and replace with teak and or marine plywood. Dad decided we needed a cabin to fend off the weather and make it more comfortable and that became what seemed as an endless proposition. John and I were relegated to hand screwing a thousand brass screws and our hands looked like we had been sorting razor blades by the time the project was completed. In retrospect I think Dad could have bought a yacht for the money he dumped into his Titanic.

To complete the project Dad and George signed up for a Power Squadron course that burned most of the winter months. Spring arrived and Dad was ready for the maiden voyage and found a berth at the Erie Yacht Club to harbor our new luxury liner. Trial run went well but the engine needed work so Dad hired and marine mechanic to jump on board and fine tune the Chrysler engine. We were up and ready to join the Seventh Fleet and enjoyed fishing that summer and getting acquainted with our boat that proved to be quite sea worthy although it failed to make best in show. Now we had to redesign our techniques relative to setting the boxes that had been very proficient with the outboard and trailer, etc. It was decided that part of the team would haul the outboard and box out to the set up location and set the box and decoys in the normal fashion and then Dad would run the power boat out near the box and we would climb up onto the boat and tie the outboard to the side for retrieving ducks and handling the hunter exchange. It worked great and was very comfortable as we all awaited our turn in the box.
It was bit cumbersome hiking over the side and into the service

boat with all of our gear but it was working ok. One weekend I invited Dick Foran, my high school hunting buddy to join us in his first box hunting experience and Dick was so excited that he rushed down to the Army Surplus and bought a complete B-29 Bomber crew sheep lined suit and he was decked out head to toe and looked like Big Foot when he jumped on board.

Dad decided to move the power boat further away from the box and Dick was standing in the rear with me and when Dad gunned the power Dick flopped backwards into the bay. Luckily I was able to grab a handful of his wool legging and haul him into the boat as we were both busting a gut laughing He looked like the Pillsbury Doughboy floating in the seaweed that managed to keep him afloat. Now I want to tell you when his sheepskin suit water logged it weighed a ton .We always had plenty of extra gear on board and were able to get him changed and near the heater before he was hit with hyperthermia That story hung with us for many years and Dick and I often chatted about the moment in school and every time we told the story it grew larger with many more expletives than I dare mention. May God Bless his soul as I think about the good old days and wonder how we survived.

We stayed in the bays the first season just to get the feel of the new drill and teamwork prior to venturing out through channel into the lake. The channel from the bay to the lake was always a beast no matter the weather or time of the year and the Coast Guard had strict regulations on all craft passing through the channel and rightly so. It was always busy with large craft and taking a chance without proper gear and craft was not at the top of the things to do list.

Chapter 3

Taking on the Lake:

It was in the early nineteen fifties when we geared up to hunt the lake. Others were hunting the eastern shores of Lake Erie for sometime but we were not certain how many were towing gear through the channel as many either lived on the eastern shore or drove out and unloaded from beaches in that area.

Towing our box strapped on top our outboard proved to be a bit unnerving passing through the channel during predawn hours but we managed to get to quieter water once we cleared the east piers. The lake was calm almost as the doctor ordered with a gentile southwest wind which was perfect for the set and prevented us from having to set closer to shore.

Everything checked out, decoy lines were long enough to reach and grab bottom and we had a decent moon to work with relative to setting the box and decoys. Our timing was right on the money and it appeared that we were in for a super good day of box hunting the lake for our first effort. Once we were set I was elected to take the first hour in the box which was a bit different knowing we were a good mile offshore and in very deep water. I could hear wing beats in the predawn air and see some shadows on the horizon and coming the daylight.

Once the time was approaching shooting hours all I could see for miles was flocks of ducks at every elevation imaginable. Dad and the rest of the crew, John, Dick Foran, and our neighbor George, the sea captain, were anxiously watching the flocks from a couple of hundred yards upwind from the set with the tender alongside at the ready for quick pick ups and also hunter exchanges. I dropped two Bluebills which were collected and it was agreed that once I had my limit we would switch off and hopefully bag out before noon knowing the lake tended to rough up shortly afternoon on average. We had well over two hundred decoys set as numbers really mattered in bigger areas to attract the rafting ducks that may not even see a smaller spread in any kind of chop.I was about one hour into the hunt when the water flattened which was always a sure sign of wind change and needless to say it got my attention right away. Lake Erie is the shallowest of the Great Lakes and consequently it tends to be the roughest when the winds are right, enough so that at some point in history it broke the huge lake freighter the Edmond Fitzgerald in half.

I glanced to my left to get a fix on our power boat in case we were hit with white caps so I would know where to expect the tender to approach from for a quick pick up if necessary. All I could see was a wall of white water teeming down on me at a very high rate of speed and when it hit the box it ripped the rear anchor out of the back of the box leaving only the front anchor holding and spinning the box like a whip. I knew if the front anchor ripped out as well that I was doomed roll over in the white caps and with that thought in mind I was prepared to leave the box and try and stay afloat until Dad could make the pick up. The first wave completely covered me with icy water and the box was staying afloat thanks to some styrofoam flotation blocks that we built into false walls in the front and sides. I remember heading down the next swell and it looked like a bottomless pit. How the box ever rose up to the top of the next wave I will never know. I saw Dad trying to get into the outboard which was crazy and I waved him off and was pointing at the power boat and he got to the controls and headed right for me which was a bit creepy in that rough water but it was our only choice.

My life jacket was on and I kicked off my hip boots and was bound and determined that I would not let go of my treasured shotgun until the last moment. I did not panic in the least but had a moment or two after we were safe on shore. Dad shot right at me and cut hard left and let the boat ram into the box at which time I faulted into the boat tossing John my empty gun all in one motion.

The box went to the bottom and the outboard tender was well on its way to see the wizard and nobody cared a bit. Decoys, box and outboard all vanished in minutes and Dad looked like he was in at the middle of a bad nightmare. Without a moments hesitation he hit the throttle and headed straight for the beach yelling when we hit bottom jump and run for it. We were all cocked and ready and when we beached the cruiser we were tossed like rocks unto the beach and for safe keeping I think we ran a one hundred yards to be certain we were not dragged back into the surf. The inboard was ripped to pieces and we all reflected back on the hours we spent rebuilding her. Dad as solemn as a church mouse said, we are all alive and that is all that matters. We were up against step clay cliff and did not have a clue where the hell we were in a nasty storm but after taking inventory we all agreed with Dad, the hell with it we are all alive. If Dad tried to get back to the channel I truly doubt I would be writing this book today.

John and Dick Foran climbed the cliff and made it to a farm house and called my mother to come and pick us up.The farmer picked us up in a hay wagon and hauled us to the farm and when Mother arrived she was a wreck but was happy we all survived the ordeal. We never did retrieve a decoy, boat or motor nor did we ever look back. Dad sold the boat for salvage and that was our last attempt to hunt the lake in a box. Bear in mind we did have some rough days on the bays as well but never as nasty as the first and last day on the lake. It was collectively decided that blind hunting would be just fine and keeping the boxes in the bay also received a unanimous vote. I headed off to college that fall and then off to the Army after being drafted and it was some time before I was able to enjoy duck hunting again and needless to say it was never the same for me again. I will elaborate on the changes in my next book which is in the works as I finish this one dedicated to my Labrador Buck, "Buck Beach and Field Commander"

Closing notes:

It has been sometime since my last days of hunting on Presque Isle however the memory bank is just a fresh today as it once was during the golden years. We hunted just about every foot of bay shorelines during our prime and never experienced a disappointing day or moment even though there were days that few birds passed by our set ups. The good friends and wonderful privilege of being able to enjoy reasonably good duck hunting so close to home was in and of itself a dream come true. We hunted all of the local game lands, creeks and nearby marsh's and many other haunts but none could compare to hunting the shores of Lake Erie. To those that continue to hunt the shores of the lakes and bays stay active and give back to your chosen sport to insure perpetuation for the youngsters following in your footsteps.

Time to patch up and support the very reason you have duck hunting privileges on Presque Isle Bay

North West Penna Duck Hunters Association:

Preserve wildlife take Retriever hunting.

Good Hunting and may the Red God's smile upon you
Bruce Barber

NOTES

www.ingramcontent.com/pod-product-compliance
Ingram Content Group UK Ltd.
Pitfield, Milton Keynes, MK11 3LW, UK
UKHW041905190726
13854UKWH00003B/1095

9 781329 142053